25 ESSENTIALS

TECHNIQUES FOR
GRILLING FISH

25

ESSENTIALS

TECHNIQUES FOR

GRILLING FISH

KAREN ADLER AND
JUDITH FERTIG

The Harvard Common Press
Boston, Massachusetts

The Harvard Common Press
535 Albany Street
Boston, Massachusetts 02118
www.harvardcommonpress.com

Printed in China
Printed on acid-free paper

Library of Congress Cataloging-in-Publication Data
Adler, Karen
  25 essentials : techniques for grilling fish / Karen Adler and Judith Fertig
      p. cm.
  Includes index.
  ISBN 978-1-55832-669-9 (alk. paper)
  1. Barbecue cookery. 2. Cookery (Fish) 3. Cookery (Seafood) I. Fertig, Judith M. II. Title. III. Title: Twenty five essentials, techniques for grilling fish. IV. Title: Techniques for grilling fish. V. Title: Grilling fish.
  TX840.B3A3175 2010
  641.6'92--dc22
                                                    2009032136

Special bulk-order discounts are available on this and other Harvard Common Press books. Companies and organizations may purchase books for premiums or resale, or may arrange a custom edition, by contacting the Marketing Director at the address above.

Book design by Elizabeth Van Itallie
Photography by Joyce Oudkerk Pool
Food styling by Jen Straus, with assistance from Jason Wheeler

We'd like to thank the good folks at Monterey Fish Market, whose beautiful seafood is highlighted in the photos in these pages. Contact http://www.montereyfish.com.

10 9 8 7 6 5 4 3 2 1

CONTENTS

SHELLFISH

ACKNOWLEDGMENTS

As Midwesterners, our special acknowledgment goes to Federal Express for bringing fresh fish on a daily basis to Kansas City and other Midwestern cities, beginning in the late 1980s. It was because of FedEx that Karen's first book, *Hooked on Fish on the Grill* (Pig Out Publications, 1992), sold more than 75,000 copies regionally. Following the success of that first book, we collaborated on *Fish & Shellfish, Grilled & Smoked* (The Harvard Common Press, 2002), which is the most comprehensive book available on the subject of grilling, smoking, and planking seafood. We also want to thank you, cookbook readers and grilling enthusiasts. We wish you delicious success with every fish or shellfish that you grill!

INTRODUCTION

A question often asked of us is, "Why would two women from the Midwest write cookbooks about fish and shellfish?" Our reply: "We write books about *grilling* fish and shellfish!"

The truth is, we know our way inside and out, upside down and right-side up, of just about any grill or smoker. We are both avid indoor cooks as well, and our philosophy is that just about anything that you cook indoors can be adapted to be cooked outdoors. The big plus in cooking outdoors comes from that smoky, charred flavor that you get from using a grill.

As authors of more than 24 cookbooks, including a whopping 13 on the subject of barbecue, and with our Ph.B. degrees (Doctor of Barbecue Philosophy) from the Kansas City Barbeque Society's Greasehouse University, we want to share with you the "Wow!" factor you get when fish and shellfish are grilled. Once you learn the basics we teach you in these pages, you'll get hooked on the extraordinary flavor of all kinds of grilled seafood.

If there is one food that most people are afraid to grill, it's probably seafood. But it's really a very simple way to cook, and you'll get loads of compliments every time you do it. In *Fish & Shellfish, Grilled & Smoked* (The Harvard Common Press, 2002), we took home cooks, step by step, through the process of grilling and smoking the many luscious and tender denizens of lakes, streams, and oceans. We've also demonstrated to thousands of students in countless classes around the country how to grill-smoke, plank, stir-grill, skewer, and rotisserie-cook fish and shellfish. So put your trust in us: Grilling fish and shellfish is easy and fun, and the results are fantastic!

THE ESSENTIALS
OF GRILLING SEAFOOD

You'll want to use the highest-quality fish and shellfish you can find, which sometimes means that you'll go home with a different fish from what you set out to buy, or that you'll choose IQF (individually quick frozen) or FAS (frozen at sea) over fresh. It's important to go to a reputable market where there is a high turnover of product and establish a relationship with the fishmonger there.

We have included a fish and shellfish substitution chart (page 14) so that you can always be prepared to use the best seafood possible. For example, if you have your heart set on salmon but it's not available, you can use char or halibut instead. If all of the fresh fish looks past its prime, choose frozen fish from the freezer case, not the kind that's sold thawed in the fish case and marked as "previously frozen" (who knows how long the fish was in the freezer?). Fresh fish and shellfish should smell briny, like the sea, not like ammonia, and be somewhat firm to the touch. Whole fish should have clear eyes.

Preparing fish and shellfish for the grill or smoker is a snap: a brush of olive oil, a sprinkling of seasoning, or a marinade. Just don't marinate fish and shellfish for more than 30 minutes or you could "cook" the delicate flesh into ceviche—which is delicious but not what you want here. The only exception would be a very oily fish with a mildly acidic marinade, as in Japanese-Style Grilled Fish (page 32).

Even when the skin has been removed from a fish fillet, you can still see where it used to be. So when you're grilling fish and we tell you to start with the flesh side down, you'll know which side that is (the interior side along the backbone, which never had skin on it). Grilling fish flesh side down first makes it easier for you to keep the fillet together after you turn it on the grill.

The general rule for most fish is to grill it for 10 minutes per inch of thickness over a hot fire. Thus, if you have a typical fish fillet that measures ¾ inch at the thickest part, you should grill it for 3½ to 4 minutes on the flesh side, turn the fillet, and grill it for 3 to 4 minutes more.

The exception to the rule is meaty fish such as tuna, swordfish, and shark, which many people like to eat rare to medium. These types of fish will be well done over a hot fire in 6 to 7 minutes per inch of thickness. They are lean as well as meaty and tend to overcook and dry out more quickly than other fish. If you want a rare tuna steak, grill it for 1 to 2 minutes per side over a hot fire.

FISH SUBSTITUTION GUIDE FOR THE GRILL

The following guide will help you select the freshest fish at the market. If your first choice is not available, substitute another fish from the same category, or one category

GRILLING SHELLFISH

We like to grill shellfish quickly over high heat. Oysters on the half shell need only a few minutes—look for the edges of the oyster to curl and then pull the oysters off the grill right away. Clams and mussels cook in 3 to 5 minutes and should be removed from the grill as soon as the shells pop open. Lobster tails with the shell on need about 12 minutes. Large shrimp and sea scallops need only 6 minutes; they should be pulled off the grill when they just begin to turn opaque. They will keep cooking after they leave the grill, and we want to spare you the culinary agony of tough, dry, overcooked shellfish. Smaller shrimp and scallops need even less time.

over. Some recipes will work with almost any kind of fish, so feel free to experiment.

This guide groups fish by flavor (mild to pronounced) and by texture (firm to delicate). If you want to grill a delicate fish, we recommend using a fish basket, perforated grill rack, disposable aluminum pan, or heavy-duty aluminum foil. That way the fish won't flake and fall through the grill grate onto the fire. Keep this in mind when choosing from this category.

Names of fish can be confusing. Different markets might use the fish family name, the local or regional name, or possibly a Hawaiian, Spanish, or French name. The most common names are included here to aid you in your fish shopping.

FIRM TEXTURE	MILD FLAVOR	MODERATE FLAVOR	FULL FLAVOR
	Barramundi	Clams	Cuttlefish
	Blackfish	Cobia (Sargent Fish)	Escolar
	Halibut	Drum (White Sea Bass)	Marlin (A'u)
	John Dory (St. Peter's Fish)	Moonfish (Opah)	Mussels
	Lobster	Salmon	Octopus
	Monkfish	Shark	Oysters
	Oreo Dory	Skate	Squid
	Prawns	Striped Marlin (Nairagi)	Triggerfish
	Red Drum (Redfish)	Sturgeon	
	Sea Bass (Loup de Mer)	Swordfish	
	Shrimp	Yellowfin Tuna	
	Soft-Shell Crab		

MODERATELY FIRM TEXTURE	MILD FLAVOR	MODERATE FLAVOR	FULL FLAVOR
	Catfish	Arctic Char	Amberjack
	Grouper	Barracuda	Kingfish
	Ocean Perch (Redfish)	Bonito	King Mackerel
	Orange Roughy	Mahi-Mahi (Dorado)	Mackerel
	Pompano	Sablefish (Black Cod)	Mullet
	Sea Scallops	Sea Bream (Daurade)	Permit
	Snapper	Sea Trout (Weakfish)	Wahoo (Ono)
	Striped Bass	Tilapia	Yellowtail Jack (Hamachi)
	Walleye	Trout	Yellowtail Snapper
	Whitefish		

DELICATE TEXTURE	MILD FLAVOR	MODERATE FLAVOR	FULL FLAVOR
	Bass (freshwater)	Herring	Anchovy
	Cod	Pomfret (Butterfish, Dollarfish)	Bluefish
	Crappie (freshwater)	Shad	Buffalo Fish
	Flounder	Smelt (Whitebait)	Sardine
	Hake (Whiting)		
	Pink Snapper (Opakapaka)		

FIRE UP!

Starting a good fire is the first step to grilling succulent fish and shellfish. Here's how to do it.

CHARCOAL GRILLS

Charcoal fires can be started in any of several safe, ecologically sound ways. We like using hardwood charcoal because it is natural and gives a better wood flavor, but we also use charcoal briquets or a combination of hardwood charcoal and briquets. If you like, mix them together, as many of our barbecue-competition buddies do. Hardwood charcoal is available at some grocery stores, as well as at hardware, barbecue, and home-improvement stores. Briquets are more readily available at grocery stores, convenience shops, and hardware and home-improvement stores.

Choices for lighting a charcoal fire include using a charcoal chimney, an electric fire starter, or lighter fluid. The charcoal chimney is an upright cylindrical metal canister, like a large metal coffee can with a handle. Fill the top of the chimney with hardwood lump charcoal and/or briquets. Place the chimney on a nonflammable surface, such as concrete or the grill rack. Slightly tip the chimney over and stuff one to two sheets of crumpled newspaper in the convex-shaped bottom. Light the paper with a match. After 5 minutes, check to make sure that the fire is still going. If not, stuff with paper and light again. The coals should be red hot and starting to ash over in 15 to 20 minutes. Carefully dump the coals onto the bottom of the grill grate, and add more charcoal if needed. You can also use the charcoal chimney to add coals if you're grilling something over a low fire for a longer time.

To use an electric fire starter, place it on the bottom grill grate. Mound the charcoal on top and plug it in. The coals will take about 15 minutes to ignite. Carefully remove the starter and set it in a safe place to cool.

Lighter fluid, a petroleum product, can impart an unpleasant flavor if improperly used. Used correctly, however, it will not impart any flavor to your food. Douse the charcoal with lighter fluid according to the manufacturer's directions and light with a match. Don't start to grill until the coals have burned down to an ashen coating over glowing embers. That way, any petroleum residue will be burned off.

Gas Grills

Follow your manufacturer's directions for starting your gas grill. This will include attaching the propane tank to the grill, turning on the propane valve, then lighting the burners of the gas grill. About 40,000 combined BTUs (British Thermal Units, which measure the maximum heat output of a burner) are optimum. Many grills have thermometers attached to the grill lid, so close the lid and let it heat up to the desired temperature.

Fueling the Fire

Now that you've got your fire, you need to maintain and manage it for cooking over direct or indirect heat. Here's how.

Techniques for Cooking on Charcoal Grills

DIRECT FIRE. After you have started the fire, wait until the charcoal is red hot and beginning to ash over before putting on the oiled grill grate. Place food on the grill grate directly over the hot coals. Leave the grill lid open or closed, depending on the recipe. If you need to add more coals, ignite them in the charcoal chimney first.

CAST IRON GRILLING. You use a cast iron skillet or griddle over direct heat. Again, the cast iron needs to get very, very hot; when properly heated, the cast iron should have a grayish cast. You oil the food, not the griddle.

INDIRECT FIRE. Prepare a direct fire first. Once you have your hot coals on the fire grate, push the coals over to the side of the grill. One side of the grill will have hot coals—that is the direct heat cooking side. The other side will not have hot coals—that is the indirect-heat cooking side.

TECHNIQUES FOR COOKING ON GAS GRILLS

DIRECT FIRE. Turn the burners on. Place the food on the grill grate directly over the hot burner, and that is direct heat. To cook this way, you can either leave the grill lid up or down.

CAST IRON GRILLING. You use a cast iron skillet or griddle over direct heat. Again, the cast iron needs to get very, very hot, with the cast iron taking on a grayish cast. You oil the food, not the griddle.

INDIRECT FIRE. Light the burners on one half of the grill only. The side of the grill without the burners on is the indirect heat side. To cook this way, you must close the grill lid.

Now, let's go to our first Essential!

25
ESSENTIALS

TECHNIQUES FOR
GRILLING FISH

SALT AND PEPPER-GRILLED FILLETS WITH HOMEMADE TARTAR SAUCE

SERVES 4

There are two factors to consider when grilling great fish fillets. The first is your choice of fillet. If you're a beginner, start with farm-raised catfish because it's mild-flavored yet fairly firm in texture, so it holds together well on the grill. Then move on to salmon, halibut, sea bass, and the rest of the big world of fish. Once you get the hang of grilling fish, try delicate varieties like freshwater bass or cod. Just use an oiled perforated grill rack and two large fish spatulas to turn the fillets once during grilling. You may grill fish with or without the skin on—just always begin grilling on the flesh side then finish on the skin side (whether there is skin or not), because the skin side holds together better and it will be easier to remove the fish from the grill without falling apart.

The second factor to consider involves heat and timing. Grill fish fillets for 10 minutes per inch of thickness (judged by the thickest part of the fillet) over a hot fire. A catfish fillet, for example, is usually about ¾ inch thick in the thickest part. That means you should grill the fillet for about 7 minutes total, turning once halfway through.

INGREDIENTS

HOMEMADE TARTAR SAUCE

1 cup mayonnaise

$\frac{1}{4}$ cup sweet pickle relish

2 tablespoons grated onion

2 teaspoons fresh lemon juice

1 teaspoon Worcestershire sauce

Kosher or sea salt and freshly ground black pepper to taste

4 fish fillets, 5 to 6 ounces each

Olive oil

Kosher or sea salt and freshly ground black pepper to taste

METHOD

1. Prepare a hot fire in a grill. Oil the grill grate or a perforated grill rack.

2. To make the tartar sauce, mix all the ingredients in a small bowl until well blended. Cover and refrigerate until serving time. (Tartar sauce can be made up to 2 days ahead of time.)

3. Brush or spray the fillets on both sides with olive oil. Place the fish, flesh side down, on the grill rack and grill for 10 minutes per inch of thickness, turning once halfway through. A fish fillet is done when it begins to flake when tested with a fork in the thickest part.

4. Remove from the grill, season with salt and pepper, and serve hot with the tartar sauce.

LIME-GRILLED SWORDFISH WITH FIRE-ROASTED SALSA

SERVES 4

Fish fillets are cut along the backbone, on either side of the fish, yielding two long fillets per fish. Fish steaks, however, are cut across the fish, leaving the backbone and pin bones in the middle; they may or may not have the skin still on them. They are usually cut from larger fish such as swordfish, halibut, tuna, or salmon. If swordfish is not available in your area, substitute any of these other fish steaks. The "10 minutes per inch of thickness" rule applies to fish steaks as well as to fillets, so measure your fish steak and grill accordingly, turning once. Because of the uniform thickness of a steak, it cooks more evenly, holds together better, and is easier to turn than a fillet.

We slather these fish steaks with a fresh-tasting grilling paste that acts like a marinade, and then grill them over a hot fire. You might be tempted to eat all of the salsa with tortilla chips, but be sure to save some to serve with the luscious lime-grilled fish.

INGREDIENTS

FIRE-ROASTED SALSA

1 cup canned chopped fire-roasted tomatoes, with juice

1 canned chipotle chile in adobo sauce, patted dry and finely chopped

$\frac{1}{4}$ cup finely chopped red onion

$\frac{1}{4}$ cup finely chopped fresh cilantro

2 teaspoons fresh lime juice

Kosher or sea salt and freshly ground black pepper to taste

3 tablespoons fresh lime juice

3 tablespoons olive oil

2 cloves garlic, minced

4 swordfish steaks, 8 ounces each (about 1 inch thick)

METHOD

1. Prepare a hot fire in a grill.

2. To make the salsa, combine all the ingredients in a medium bowl. Set aside.

3. Combine the lime juice, olive oil, and garlic in a small bowl. Rub the mixture over the swordfish steaks.

4. Place the fish on the grill and cook for 10 minutes per inch of thickness, turning once halfway through. A fish steak is done when it begins to flake when tested with a fork in the center.

5. Serve hot, accompanied by the salsa.

CILANTRO-BUTTERED TROUT WITH YELLOW TOMATO CONSERVE

SERVES 4

Why not try grilling a whole fish? You'll end up with a moist, succulent, tender fish with the flavor of the grill. Our favorite whole fish to grill are freshwater trout and ocean fish such as mackerel or bluefish. If you're buying a whole fish, the proof of freshness is in the eyes—of the beholder and the fish. A fresh fish's eyes should be clear and brilliant, not cloudy. A whole fish bought at the store should already be cleaned and scaled for you; if in doubt, ask.

Whole fish can be grilled in a hinged wire basket, which prevents the fish from falling through the grill grates and keeps any herb or butter mixture inside the cavity of the fish. You can also put the fish directly on the grill grates and turn them once during cooking. Or arrange the fish on an oiled, perforated grill rack set right on the grill grates.

Use an indirect fire—a medium-hot to hot fire on one side and no fire on the other side. This way, you can move the fish to the indirect side if the exterior starts to get too blackened. For whole fish measuring about 1½ inches in the thickest part, this translates to 14 to 15 minutes cooking time plus another 5 minutes for the backbone.

INGREDIENTS

YELLOW TOMATO CONSERVE

2 cups chopped ripe yellow tomatoes

$\frac{1}{4}$ cup chopped scallions (white parts with some of the green)

3 banana peppers, stemmed, seeded, and diced

$\frac{1}{4}$ cup bottled Italian dressing

$\frac{1}{4}$ teaspoon red pepper flakes

2 lemons, sliced

4 sprigs fresh cilantro, plus 1 tablespoon chopped

4 cleaned whole trout, 14 to 16 ounces each

Kosher or sea salt and freshly ground black pepper

$\frac{1}{2}$ cup (1 stick) unsalted butter

2 tablespoons fresh lemon juice

METHOD

1. Prepare an indirect fire in a grill, with a hot fire on one side and no fire on the other. Oil the grill grate.

2. To make the tomato conserve, combine all the ingredients in a medium bowl. Cover and refrigerate until ready to serve.

3. Place 2 or 3 slices of lemon and a cilantro sprig in the cavity of each fish and season with salt and pepper. In a saucepan, melt the butter; stir in the chopped cilantro and the lemon juice. Keep warm.

4. Place the fish on the grill grate over the hot fire. Grill for about 10 minutes per side, basting occasionally with the cilantro-butter mixture and turning once halfway through. Move to the indirect side for a bit if the fish begins to blacken, then move back to direct heat.

5. Season with salt and pepper and serve hot with any extra cilantro butter, accompanied by the tomato conserve.

JAPANESE-STYLE GRILLED FISH

SERVES 4

Most freshwater and ocean fish can be marinated for only 30 minutes at most—or they turn opaque and are essentially "cooked" before you even go out to the grill. The exception, though, is strong-flavored, oily fish like amberjack, bluefish, salmon, mackerel, marlin, mullet, or even our old standby, farm-raised catfish, which can stand up to longer marinating. In fact, marinating these oily fish for a longer time makes them taste even better.

Our Japanese-style marinade is not too acidic—it's the acid from citrus juices or vinegar that can "pickle" fish in minutes. Soy sauce and sake add a spirited flavor. Sugar and mirin, a sweet Japanese wine, give a glazed appearance to the finished dish. And fresh ginger makes it all come together.

INGREDIENTS

JAPANESE-STYLE MARINADE

$\frac{1}{4}$ cup soy sauce

$\frac{1}{4}$ cup sake or dry white wine

$\frac{1}{4}$ cup mirin or sweet sherry

2 tablespoons sugar

2 tablespoons grated fresh ginger

4 fish fillets (bluefish, mackerel, or other oily fish), about 6 ounces each

Olive oil

Kosher or sea salt and freshly ground black pepper to taste

Lemon slices for serving

METHOD

1. To make the marinade, combine all the ingredients in a small saucepan. Bring to a boil over medium-high heat, and then immediately remove from the heat. Cover and let cool to room temperature.

2. Arrange the fish fillets in a deep baking dish and pour the marinade over. Cover and refrigerate for 4 hours or overnight, turning the fish occasionally.

3. Prepare a hot fire in a grill. Oil the grill grate or a perforated grill rack.

4. Remove the fish from the marinade and pat dry. Brush or spray the fillets on both sides with olive oil. Place the fish, flesh side down, on the grill rack and grill for 10 minutes per inch of thickness, turning once halfway through. A fish fillet is done when it begins to flake when tested with a fork in the thickest part. Remove from the grill, season with salt and pepper, and serve hot, garnished with fresh lemon slices.

GRILLED TILAPIA WITH SPICY LEMON PEPPER RUB

SERVES 4

You see those thin, delicious-looking fillets glistening on the chipped ice in the fishmonger's case. Oh no, you think, too thin to grill. The day is saved, however, if you have a perforated grill rack—like a metal cookie sheet with holes punched in it. Make sure the thin fillets are not too delicate in texture like Dover sole, but more like snapper, cod, or flounder. (Moderate to firm fillets may not even need the grill rack.) Simply oil the grill rack and, for double insurance, oil the fish fillets, too, and the grilling will be easy.

On a perforated grill rack, a fish fillet about ½ inch thick should be done in 5 minutes, about 2½ minutes per side. If your fillet is thinner than ½ inch, do not attempt to turn it; instead simply grill it with the lid closed so both sides get done at the same time.

Very thin fish fillets are usually very delicate in flavor, too, so you can go one of two ways with the accompaniments: Provide a contrast with a spicy, lemony dry rub and finish with a little melted lemon-butter drizzle, as we do, or complement their delicacy with just a little butter and lemon juice.

Last, thin delicate fillets are also perfect for planking. See Planking Fish Fillets on page 52.

INGREDIENTS

SPICY LEMON PEPPER RUB

¼ cup lemon pepper seasoning

1 tablespoon chili powder

1 tablespoon ground cumin

1 tablespoon ground coriander

1½ teaspoons firmly packed light or dark brown sugar

½ teaspoon kosher or coarse sea salt

½ teaspoon red pepper flakes

1¼ teaspoons freshly ground black pepper

4 tilapia fillets, about 6 ounces each

Olive oil

Kosher or sea salt and freshly ground black pepper to taste

½ cup (1 stick) unsalted butter, melted

2 tablespoons fresh lemon juice

METHOD

1. Prepare a hot fire in a grill. Oil the grill grate and a perforated grill rack.

2. To make the rub, combine all the ingredients in a small jar with a tight-fitting lid. Secure the lid and shake to blend.

3. Brush or spray the fillets on both sides with olive oil and sprinkle each fillet with about 1 teaspoon of the rub. (Save the rest for later use; it will keep in the cupboard for several months.) Place the fish, flesh side down, on the oiled perforated grill rack and grill for 10 minutes per inch of thickness, turning once halfway through. A fish fillet is done when it begins to flake when tested with a fork in the thickest part. Remove from the grill and season with salt and pepper. Combine the melted butter and lemon juice and drizzle the lemon butter over the grilled fish. Serve hot.

STIR-GRILLED SALMON WITH CHERRY TOMATOES AND SUGAR SNAP PEAS

SERVES 4

Stir-grilling fish and vegetables is simplicity itself. All you need are fish fillet strips and veggies cut into small pieces, a zipper-top plastic bag, a marinade of some kind, a perforated grill wok, wooden stir-grilling paddles or grill spatulas, and a grill. You just marinate the fish and veggies in the bag, and then pour the contents of the bag into the grill wok, which is placed over the sink (or in the grass outside) to avoid a mess. Then you cook the mixture on the grill, stirring, until the food is done to your liking.

You'll be amazed at the extra flavor stir-grilling can impart to the most basic of foods. Once you've tried this recipe, get creative and try other tender vegetables, such as bell peppers, zucchini, yellow summer squash, mushrooms, onions of all kinds, and more.

Do not slice the fish or vegetables too thinly, or they may fall through the holes in the grill wok. And be sure to fill the wok no higher than halfway so that you have room to stir and turn the vegetables with the paddles. Serve over rice or inside flour tortillas for an Asian-style wrap.

INGREDIENTS

ASIAN MARINADE

¼ cup soy sauce

¼ cup rice wine vinegar

2 tablespoons honey

4 cloves garlic, minced

1 teaspoon freshly grated ginger

1 teaspoon tahini

1 pound salmon fillets, cut into 2-inch pieces

½ pound sugar snap peas, stemmed

12 cherry or grape tomatoes

½ red onion, sliced ½-inch thick

METHOD

1. To make the marinade, combine all the ingredients in a large zipper-top plastic bag. Add the salmon, snap peas, tomatoes, and onion. Seal the bag and toss to coat. Marinate for 30 to 45 minutes in the refrigerator.

2. Prepare a hot fire in a grill.

3. Coat a 12- or 15-inch grill wok with nonstick cooking spray on both sides. Over the sink, dump the marinated salmon and vegetables into the oiled grill wok and let any excess marinade drain off. Set the wok on a baking tray to carry out to the grill. Place the wok directly over the fire and stir-grill, tossing with wooden paddles or grill spatulas every few minutes, until the fish is opaque and just firm to the touch, 8 to 10 minutes. Close the lid for 3 to 4 minutes to heat everything all the way through, especially if the outdoor temperature is a bit cool. Serve hot.

BAJA-STYLE FISH TACOS
SERVES 4

This lighter, fresher cousin of the beef taco comes from the Baja peninsula on the Pacific Ocean. Served with a tangy, herby slaw in flour tortillas, a fish taco is delicious with a margarita or a chilled Mexican beer and a wedge of lime.

The traditional fish taco features fish that is dipped in a batter and fried, sometimes paired with a vinegary red cabbage slaw. But we love the even lighter, fresher flavor of grilled fish in tacos. You'll want a fish with a mild flavor and a delicate to medium-delicate texture, such as halibut, orange roughy, red snapper, monkfish, or cod. Use fillets with the skin still on so they will hold together better on the grill. Grill them flesh side down first, turn once with two wide fish spatulas, and then finish grilling skin side down. You can serve the grilled fillet, skin side down, on a platter and let guests help themselves. It's easy to break the tender fish into chunks with a fork, leaving the skin behind.

INGREDIENTS

NAPA CABBAGE SLAW

2 cups shredded Napa cabbage

1 cup shredded baby greens, such as escarole, oak leaf lettuce, spinach, or
Bibb lettuce

6 scallions, finely chopped (white parts with some of the green)

$\frac{1}{4}$ cup tarragon vinegar

$\frac{1}{4}$ cup sour cream

Juice of 2 lemons

$\frac{1}{2}$ teaspoon kosher or coarse sea salt

$1\frac{1}{2}$ pounds halibut, red snapper, or orange roughy fillets, with skin on

Olive oil

2 to 3 tablespoons Spicy Lemon Pepper Rub (page 38)

8 flour tortillas, warmed

Lemon wedges for serving

$1\frac{1}{2}$ cups prepared salsa of your choice, for serving

METHOD

1. Prepare a hot fire in a grill. Oil the grill grate or a perforated grill rack.

2. To make the slaw, combine the cabbage, greens, and scallions in a large bowl. Whisk the vinegar, sour cream, lemon juice, and salt together in a small bowl. Toss the greens with the dressing. Cover and refrigerate if not serving right away; bring to room temperature before serving. (Slaw can be made up to 2 days ahead of time.)

3. Brush or spray the fillets on both sides with olive oil. Sprinkle with the rub. Place the fish, flesh side down, on the grill rack and grill for 10 minutes per inch of thickness, turning once halfway through. A fish fillet is done when it begins to flake when tested with a fork in the thickest part. Remove from the grill.

4. To make the tacos, break the fish into chunks. Place 4 to 5 chunks in the center of each tortilla, top with about ⅓ cup slaw, and roll up. Serve with lemon wedges and salsa on the side.

ASIAN TUNA BURGERS WITH WASABI MAYO

SERVES 6

In *The Great Big Burger Book* (The Harvard Common Press, 2003), Jane Murphy and Liz Yeh Singh offer a huge range of burgers, from ground meats to steak sandwiches, with some delicious vegetarian options as well. We love this recipe, which is also delicious made with salmon or shrimp.

For a fish burger, you'll need a medium-hot fire. Grill the burgers for 5 to 7 minutes per side, turning just once, as seafood burgers can be delicate. If you're feeling a bit nervous, place them on an oiled, perforated grill rack to grill them. You want the burgers to be juicy, so take care not to overcook them. If they're still a little rare for your taste, you can always put them back on the grill to sizzle a little longer. But if they're overdone, there is no remedy.

INGREDIENTS

WASABI MAYO

¼ cup plus 2 tablespoons mayonnaise

3 tablespoons finely chopped scallions (white parts with some of the green)

2 teaspoons grated fresh ginger

2 teaspoons soy sauce

1 teaspoon wasabi paste or powder

One 12-ounce tuna steak or fillet, cut into ¼-inch dice, skin and any
   bones discarded

2 cloves garlic, minced

2 teaspoons grated fresh ginger

1 tablespoon toasted sesame oil

3 tablespoons soy sauce

¼ cup finely chopped scallions (white parts with some of the green)

½ teaspoon kosher or coarse sea salt

¼ teaspoon freshly ground black pepper

6 sesame seed buns, cut in half and toasted

1 cup fresh mizuna or other baby Asian greens

METHOD

1. Prepare a medium-hot fire in a grill. Oil the grill grate or a perforated grill rack.

2. To make the wasabi mayo, combine all the ingredients in a food processor and process until smooth. Taste and adjust the seasonings. Transfer to a bowl, cover, and refrigerate. (Wasabi mayo can be made 1 day ahead of time.)

3. Combine the tuna, garlic, ginger, sesame oil, soy sauce, scallions, salt, and pepper in a large bowl. Form the mixture into six 1-inch-thick patties.

4. Grill the burgers until browned on both sides and cooked to the desired degree of doneness (the middle can still be reddish pink), 5 to 7 minutes total.

5. To assemble and serve the burgers, place each burger on a toasted sesame seed bun and top with the wasabi mayo and mizuna.

PLANKED SALMON WITH MUSTARD-MAYO-DILL SLATHER

SERVES 6

Planking fish or shellfish is one of the easiest, most foolproof ways to grill seafood. The fish won't fall through the grill grate, and you don't have to turn it. This technique is perfect for delicate fillets like fresh-water bass and crappie. You can plank almost any fish or shellfish, but for the best outcome, choose varieties that are not more than 1 inch thick, so that you get more flavor from the wood underneath. For maximum flavor, the flesh should touch the wood plank, so purchase skinless fish or skin it yourself. With planking, as with grilling, the thickness of the fish (measured at the thickest part) determines the timing. A ¾-inch-thick fillet will take 25 to 30 minutes using this indirect method.

Planking fish adds two flavors: the aromatic wood flavor of the plank (usually cedar or alder for fish) on the bottom of the fish fillet and the flavor of the grill on the top. The slather ensures that you'll have a moist finished dish.

There are many ways to plank—over direct heat, over indirect heat, or using dual heat. The most common way to plank fish uses an indirect fire, meaning that only one side of the grill is hot. You put a presoaked plank with the food arranged on it over the no-heat side, close the lid, and cook.

INGREDIENTS

MUSTARD-MAYO-DILL SLATHER

$\frac{1}{2}$ cup Dijon mustard

$\frac{1}{2}$ cup mayonnaise

1 teaspoon chopped fresh dill

1 clove garlic, minced

Zest and juice of $\frac{1}{2}$ lemon

One $\frac{3}{4}$-inch-thick salmon fillet, $1\frac{1}{2}$ to 2 pounds, skin removed

One 15 x 6$\frac{1}{2}$ x $\frac{3}{8}$-inch cedar or alder grilling plank, soaked in water for at
   least 1 hour

METHOD

1. Prepare an indirect fire in a grill, with a hot fire on one side and no fire on the other.

2. To make the slather, combine all the ingredients in a small bowl until smooth.

3. Compare the length of the plank with the length of the salmon fillet and trim the salmon to fit the plank, if necessary. Place the salmon on the prepared plank and spread the mustard slather over the top.

4. Place the plank on the grill grate on the no-heat side. Cover the grill and cook until the fish begins to flake when tested with a fork in the thickest part, 25 to 30 minutes. Serve the salmon hot, right from the plank.

CARIBBEAN GROUPER ON SUGARCANE SKEWERS

SERVES 6

S kewering fish on all kinds of sticks, from traditional wooden skewers to rosemary, lavender, or lemongrass stalks or even sugarcane, is a great way to enjoy grilled fish with a gorgeous presentation. Wooden skewers, which come in packages at the grocery store, need to be soaked in water for at least 30 minutes before threading them with food and grilling. After grilling, you just throw the charred skewers away.

Kabob baskets—some long and cylindrical, others wide and flat to hold several metal skewers at a time—are a good choice if you like to grill skewers a lot and want more control when grilling. You need to spray or brush the baskets with oil before grilling so the food doesn't stick. When you're ready to turn the skewers, you just flip the entire basket.

If you love Caribbean rum drinks, you'll love the flavor this marinade imparts. Look for fresh green sugarcane at Hispanic markets, better grocery stores, or even Target. The fresh cane adds an island flair and can be cut with a sharp knife into thinner shards for skewering. Use mild- to medium-flavored, medium-textured fish here, such as farm-raised catfish, red snapper, halibut, or grouper.

INGREDIENTS

CARIBBEAN MARINADE

¼ cup light rum

¼ cup fresh lime juice (from 4 to 5 limes)

¼ cup olive oil

2 cloves garlic, minced

1 tablespoon minced shallot

1½ pounds grouper fillets, skin removed

12 slender spikes of fresh sugarcane, at least 6 inches long, soaked in water for at
least 30 minutes before grilling

METHOD

1. To make the marinade, combine all the ingredients in a small bowl.

2. Lay out the fillets so the grain of the fish is horizontal. Using a pizza wheel or chef's knife, cut the fillets against the grain into 2-inch-wide strips. Place in a bowl and pour the marinade over. Cover and refrigerate for 30 minutes.

3. Prepare a hot fire in a grill. Oil the grill grate or a kabob basket.

4. Thread the fish pieces onto the sugarcane skewers, weaving the pieces in and out and leaving space between them. Grill for 2 to 3 minutes per side, turning once. Serve hot.

HERB-GRILLED JOHN DORY WITH ROSEMARY AIOLI

SERVES 4

Grilling fish over fresh herb leaves and woody stalks is an aromatic tradition from the Mediterranean. Three herbs that develop woody stalks ideal for this purpose are thyme, rosemary, and lavender. Grilling your fish with the grill lid closed helps capture the smoky-herb flavor.

John Dory, also known as St. Peter's Fish, is a firm-textured fish from the Mediterranean with mild flavor. Feel free to substitute farm-raised catfish, monkfish, salmon, haddock, cod, or whatever is freshest at your fishmonger's. Just remember to measure the fish in the thickest part of the fillet and grill it accordingly, 10 minutes per inch of thickness. To further heighten the flavor, brush the fish with olive oil using an herb basting brush.

INGREDIENTS

ROSEMARY AIOLI

1 cup mayonnaise

2 tablespoons fresh lemon juice

2 teaspoons grated lemon zest

2 cloves garlic, minced

1 to 2 tablespoons chopped fresh rosemary, to your taste

Kosher or sea salt to taste

4 John Dory fillets, 5 to 6 ounces each

Olive oil

6 large fresh or dried thyme, rosemary, or lavender branches bundled together to make an herb basting brush

Kosher or sea salt and freshly ground black pepper to taste

METHOD

1. Prepare a hot fire in a grill. Oil the grill grate or a perforated grill rack.

2. To make the aioli, whisk all the ingredients together in a small bowl. Cover and refrigerate until serving time. (Aioli can be made up to 3 days head of time.)

3. Brush the fillets on both sides with olive oil using the herb basting brush. If you're using charcoal, place the herb basting brush right on the hot coals. If you're using a gas grill, wrap the herbs in aluminum foil, poke holes in the top of the packet, and place it near the gas jets or as close to the heat source as you can get. When you see the herby smoke waft upward from the herbs or foil packet, place the fish, flesh side down, on the grill rack, close the lid, and grill for 3 to 4 minutes per side, turning once halfway through. A fish fillet is done when it begins to flake when tested with a fork in the thickest part.

4. Season with salt and pepper and serve hot with the aioli.

COD IN A FOIL PACKET

SERVES 4

Foil-wrapping a fish fillet with other aromatic ingredients is the grill version of the "en papillote" technique of baking ingredients wrapped in parchment paper. Heavy-duty aluminum foil replaces the parchment paper, as the paper would burn up on the grill. The trick here is trying to keep the grill temperature as close to 450°F as you can get it. On a charcoal grill, you'll need a grill thermometer. Open the baffles on a charcoal grill to get more air in and thus create more heat; close the baffles to reduce the heat.

You can use just about any fish fillet with this recipe, so go with what's freshest—and about ¾ inch thick, so the timing will be the same. Pompano, grouper, bluefish, red snapper, halibut, or farm-raised catfish fillets would be good alternative choices.

Now, you won't get grill marks on the fish or the caramelized flavor of the grill, but you will have a wonderful, aromatic, moist, and delicious meal. We recommend a good, crusty bread to mop up the juices, along with a chilled Pinot Grigio or Chardonnay to toast a good-for-you dinner that's easy on the barbecuer.

INGREDIENTS

Four 18 x 18-inch sheets heavy-duty aluminum foil

4 cod fillets, 5 to 6 ounces each

1 cup sliced fresh mushrooms

1 cup canned diced Italian plum tomatoes, drained

$\frac{1}{4}$ cup chopped fresh tarragon

$\frac{1}{4}$ cup chopped fresh flat-leaf parsley

$\frac{1}{4}$ cup dry white wine

$\frac{1}{4}$ cup extra-virgin olive oil

METHOD

1. Prepare a hot fire in a grill. You'll want the temperature to be as close to 450°F as you can get it.

2. Lay each sheet of foil on a flat surface and place a fish fillet in the middle. Top each with ¼ cup of sliced mushrooms, ¼ cup of tomatoes, and 1 tablespoon each of tarragon, parsley, white wine, and olive oil. Wrap and crimp the foil to form 4 sealed packets. (The fish can be prepared to this point and refrigerated for up to 1 day, if you wish.)

3. Grill, seam side up, with the grill lid down, for 14 to 16 minutes. Do not turn.

4. To serve, place a packet on each plate, let cool slightly, and then open. If you wish, you can transfer the contents to the plate and discard the foil, or simply eat, very casually, from the foil itself.

DOWN-UNDER GRILLED BARRAMUNDI WITH LIME-GINGER MARINADE

SERVES 4

Marinating a fish fillet imbues it with great flavor. Since most marinades are fairly acidic, however, you don't want to marinate fish for longer than 30 minutes, unless it's an oily fish like bluefish, marlin, mackerel, or salmon. The acid in most marinades can "cook" non-oily fish into ceviche. Pineapple and papaya contain tenderizing enzymes that can reduce your fish to jelly in no time, so avoid using these fruit juices in your marinades.

To achieve a flavored fish fillet grilled to a moist doneness, use big, bold flavors in your fish marinades, like citrus juices, garlic, herbs and spices, fresh ginger, bottled hot sauce, rum, Grand Marnier, and tequila. Whether or not you pat your fish dry after removing it from the marinade is up to you. A little extra marinade will burn off on the grill and keep your fillet a little moister, but a lot of extra marinade will make it more difficult to get good grill marks on your fish fillets.

If barramundi is not available, substitute halibut, sea bass, salmon, monkfish, or whatever mild- to medium-flavored, medium- to firm-textured fish is freshest.

INGREDIENTS

LIME-GINGER MARINADE

¼ cup fresh lime juice (from 4 to 5 limes)

2 tablespoons vegetable oil

1 teaspoon Dijon mustard

1 teaspoon grated fresh ginger

¼ teaspoon cayenne pepper

¼ teaspoon freshly ground black pepper

4 barramundi fillets, 4 to 5 ounces each

Kosher or sea salt and freshly ground black pepper to taste

METHOD

1. To make the marinade, whisk all the ingredients together in a bowl. Arrange the fish fillets in a deep baking dish and pour the marinade over. Cover and refrigerate for 30 minutes, turning the fish two or three times.

2. Prepare a hot fire in a grill. Oil the grill grate or a perforated grill rack.

3. Remove the fish from the marinade and pat dry if desired. Place the fish, flesh side down, over the hot fire for 10 minutes per inch of thickness, turning once halfway through. A fish fillet is done when it begins to flake when tested with a fork in the thickest part.

4. Remove from the grill, season with salt and pepper, and serve hot.

VENETIAN-STYLE GRILLED LOBSTER

SERVES 8

Grilling lobster can seem daunting at first, but it's essentially easy. Just make sure to take a cooler full of ice with you to the store for transporting the lobster back to your home.

You buy lobsters live, but it's just not right to put them on the grill alive. We prefer to have the fishmonger take care of the initial lobster preparation for this dish. But you must cook the halved lobster within an hour or so of cutting it because of the rate of bacteria growth on dead lobster. If you prefer, plunge live lobsters into boiling water for 2 or 3 minutes to kill and parcook them, then cut them in half.

The Venetian method for grilling lobster is simple: Brush both halves of each lobster with olive oil and grill, flesh side down, for 3 to 4 minutes, or until you see grill marks. Turn with grill tongs to cook on the shell side until the flesh is opaque all the way through. If you parboil the lobsters first, the grilling time will be cut in half. Serve hot, in the shell, with a drizzle of extra-virgin olive oil, a squeeze of fresh lemon juice, and a sprinkling of chopped fresh flat-leaf parsley. Of course, if you have your heart set on drawn butter with your lobster, who are we to deny you?

INGREDIENTS

8 lobsters, 1¼ to 1½ pounds each

Extra-virgin olive oil

Kosher or sea salt and freshly ground black pepper to taste

½ cup chopped fresh flat-leaf parsley

2 lemons, quartered, for serving

METHOD

1. Prepare an indirect fire in a grill, with a hot fire on one side and no fire on the other. Oil the grill grates.

2. Have the fishmonger cut the lobsters in half lengthwise and remove the vein and sac from the head, or do it yourself with a chef's knife.

3. Brush both sides of the lobsters with oil. Place the lobsters, cut side down, on the hot-fire side of the grill for 4 or 5 minutes, or until you see grill marks. Turn the lobsters over and cook until the flesh is firm and white, another 3 to 4 minutes. If the lobsters are not done, move to the indirect side of the grill and continue to cook for several more minutes, until the desired doneness is reached. Do not overcook or the meat will be rubbery. If necessary, grill the lobsters in batches, keeping the finished lobsters on a platter tented with aluminum foil to keep warm.

4. Place the lobsters flesh side up on plates or a platter, drizzle with olive oil, season to taste with salt and pepper, and sprinkle with the parsley. Serve with quartered lemons so each diner can squeeze lemon juice on the lobster, if desired.

PERNOD-BUTTERED LOBSTER TAIL ON THE GRILL

SERVES 4

Unlike whole lobster, which you buy when it's still alive, lobster tails are usually sold frozen and are often labeled "rock lobster." Rock or spiny lobsters are not true lobsters, but distant cousins, and they do not have claws. That's why you'll just have the tails to grill—there's no claw meat if there are no claws.

But this feature makes rock lobster tails easier to manage for first-time lobster grillers. Simply thaw the lobster tails, remove the membrane if necessary, and loosen the meat from the shell a little bit with a sharp knife. You don't want the lobster meat to fall out while grilling, but you also don't want to have to excavate every bite.

INGREDIENTS

PERNOD BUTTER

½ cup (1 stick) unsalted butter, softened

2 tablespoons Pernod or other anise-flavored liqueur

2 tablespoons chopped fresh tarragon

4 rock lobster tails, 8 ounces each, fresh or thawed frozen

Olive oil for brushing

Kosher or sea salt and freshly ground black pepper to taste

METHOD

1. Prepare a hot fire in a grill. Oil the grill grate.

2. To make the butter, combine all the ingredients in a small bowl until well blended. Set aside.

3. Cut the top membrane from the lobster tails and discard. Loosen the meat from the shell and brush with the olive oil. Place the lobster tails, cut side down, on the grill rack and grill for 3 to 4 minutes, or until you see grill marks. Turn the lobster tails over and cook until the flesh is firm and white, another 3 to 4 minutes.

4. Place lobster tails, flesh side up, on plates or a platter, spread with the soft Pernod butter, season with salt and pepper, and serve.

WOOD-GRILLED OYSTERS IN CHIPOTLE VINAIGRETTE

SERVES 6

It used to be that you could buy and eat oysters only in months with an "R" in them. That's because during the summer months of spawning, wild oysters develop an "off" flavor. Transporting oysters in hot weather, before the days of refrigerated trucks, was also problematic. Today, about 80 percent of oysters are farm-raised in submerged nets, dining on plankton in carefully controlled marine environments. They spawn at different times during the year, so there's always a variety available that's good to eat. When ready, they're harvested and shipped by air to seafood markets. If you're not comfortable shucking oysters at home, have the fishmonger shuck them for you and ask him or her to give you a half shell for each oyster.

In this recipe, you'll get smoky flavor from two sources: the wood-grilling technique and the chipotle chile in the vinaigrette.

INGREDIENTS

CHIPOTLE VINAIGRETTE

3 tablespoons sherry vinegar

1 tablespoon balsamic vinegar

2 cloves garlic, minced

2 canned chipotle chiles in adobo sauce, very finely chopped

2 tablespoons adobo sauce from the can

$\frac{1}{2}$ teaspoon salt

$\frac{2}{3}$ cup olive oil

Freshly ground black pepper to taste

36 oysters, shucked, on the half shell

1 cup hickory or mesquite chips soaked in water for 1 hour for a charcoal grill, or $\frac{1}{2}$ cup dry wood chips in a smoker box or an aluminum foil packet poked with holes for a gas grill

METHOD

1. Prepare a hot fire in a grill.

2. To make the vinaigrette, whisk all the ingredients in a small bowl until well blended. Set aside. (Vinaigrette can be made up to 4 days ahead of time and stored, covered, in the refrigerator.)

3. Arrange the oysters in their half shells on a large baking sheet. Spoon about 1 teaspoon vinaigrette over each oyster and bring out to the grill. Add the wood chips to the coals or place the smoker box or packet close to a gas jet on a gas grill. When you see the first wisp of smoke, quickly arrange the oysters on the grill grate. Close the lid and grill for 3 to 5 minutes or until the edges of the oysters have begun to curl.

4. Arrange the oysters on plates or a platter and serve, passing extra vinaigrette at the table.

BISTRO-STYLE MUSSELS WITH GRILLED "FRITES"

SERVES 4

This classic bistro recipe translated to the grill will increase your barbecue savoir-faire as well as show your guests that you have great taste. The only hard part is cleaning the mussels.

Mussels, clams, and other closed-shell shellfish need high heat before they'll open their shells. At the same time, you don't want the shells to burn. So, arrange them on a perforated grill rack or a grill griddle—preheated on the grill rack—close the lid, and grill just until the shells open. Don't peek too much or you'll let the heat escape and the shellfish will take longer to cook. Then, sit down to a feast of flavor. Pour a glass of chilled Chablis or your favorite Beaujolais, and it's *bon appétit!* to all.

INGREDIENTS

GRILLED FRITES

4 medium baking potatoes, peeled, each cut into 8 spears

1/4 cup olive oil

2 cloves garlic, minced

1 tablespoon finely chopped fresh flat-leaf parsley

Kosher or sea salt and freshly ground black pepper

3 pounds mussels (or clams) in the shell

3 tablespoons olive oil

2 cloves garlic, minced

1/4 cup dry white wine

2 tablespoons finely chopped mixed fresh herbs, such as tarragon, basil, chives, and flat-leaf parsley

METHOD

1. Prepare a hot fire in a grill. Heat a perforated grill rack or a grill griddle.

2. To make the frites, toss the potatoes with the olive oil, garlic, and parsley on a baking sheet or a disposable aluminum pan. Season with salt and pepper. Set aside.

3. Scrub the mussels well under cold running water, pulling off their stringy beards. Discard any mussels that are not tightly closed.

4. Heat the olive oil in a saucepan over medium heat, and sauté the garlic until golden, about 3 minutes. Stir in the wine and herbs. Remove from the heat and set aside.

5. Arrange the potato spears on the grill rack or griddle and grill, gently turning every 2 minutes or so, until the potatoes have good grill marks and are tender, about 10 minutes. Remove the potatoes to a serving bowl and arrange the mussels on the grill rack or griddle. Close the lid and grill for 4 to 5 minutes, or until the shells have opened. Immediately spoon about 1 teaspoon of the garlic, herb, and wine mixture into each opened mussel. Discard any mussels that do not open.

6. Arrange the mussels on plates or a platter and pass extra garlic, herb, and wine mixture at the table. Serve with the grilled frites.

GRILLED CRAB CAKES WITH CHILE-LIME SAUCE

SERVES 4

When a delicious crab cake meets the sizzle of the grill, you get a seaside treat with loads of flavor, enhanced by a tangy lime sauce. Splash out for the more expensive, but better tasting, lump crabmeat, often found frozen. Chill the formed crab cakes so they stay firm, and take them out to the grill only after the grill has heated up and you're ready to go.

Grilling delicate crab or other shellfish cakes requires the same technique as grilling fish burgers: using a well-oiled, preheated, perforated grill rack or grill griddle and turning the cakes just once. The more you fiddle with these mixtures—so lightly held together with egg and bread crumbs—the more likely they are to fall apart. You'll spray the cakes with olive oil and then grill them over medium-high heat, so they'll brown without getting scorched.

INGREDIENTS

CHILE-LIME SAUCE

1 cup mayonnaise

1 tablespoon ancho or chipotle chile powder

1 teaspoon minced garlic

Juice of 1 lime

1/4 cup finely chopped fresh cilantro

Kosher or sea salt and freshly ground black pepper to taste

1 pound lump crabmeat, fresh or thawed frozen

2 cups fresh bread crumbs

1 large egg, beaten

1/2 cup Worcestershire sauce

1 tablespoon Dijon mustard

1 tablespoon finely chopped fresh chives

Juice of 1 lemon

1 teaspoon hot pepper sauce

1/2 teaspoon kosher salt

1/2 teaspoon freshly cracked black pepper

Olive oil cooking spray

METHOD

1. To make the sauce, stir all the ingredients together in a medium bowl. Cover and refrigerate until ready to serve. (Sauce can be made up to 1 day ahead.)

2. To make the crab cakes, gently combine the crab, 1 cup of the bread crumbs, the egg, Worcestershire sauce, mustard, chives, lemon juice, hot pepper sauce, salt, and pepper in a large bowl. Spread the remaining 1 cup bread crumbs on a plate. Form the crab mixture into 8 balls and roll each ball in the bread crumbs. Flatten the balls into patties about 2 inches thick. Arrange the crab cakes on a baking sheet, cover with plastic wrap, and refrigerate for at least 30 minutes or up to 4 hours.

3. Prepare a medium-hot fire in a grill. Heat an oiled perforated grill rack or a grill griddle.

4. Take the crab cakes out to the grill. Spray each crab cake with olive oil cooking spray on both sides. Arrange the crab cakes on the grill rack or griddle and grill, gently turning once, until browned and cooked through, 10 to 12 minutes total.

5. Arrange 2 crab cakes on each plate and serve with a dollop of sauce.

GRILL-SEARED SCALLOPS WITH PISTACHIO-TARRAGON BROWN BUTTER

SERVES 4

Scallops are so sweet, meaty, and delicious—when they're grilled right. A little too long over the flames and they become tough and rubbery. Grill-searing scallops calls for a little trust and bravery on your part. Trust that the scallops will keep on cooking, even though they don't look done all the way through when you take them off the grill. If the scallops really aren't done enough, you can always put them back on the grill for 30 seconds or so. But if they're overcooked, there's nothing you can do.

Grill-searing outdoors replicates a chef's technique of searing over high heat indoors. Some gas grills come equipped with a drop-in griddle, which is perfect for grill-searing. You'll get that fabulous contrast of dark sheen on the exterior and pale white scallop inside. You have to pay attention, however. Large sea scallops are usually about 2 inches thick, but you might be grilling sea scallops that are smaller or larger. Once they are darkened on both sides and look almost opaque in their midsections, don't hesitate—pull them off the grill.

INGREDIENTS

PISTACHIO-TARRAGON BROWN BUTTER

$\frac{1}{2}$ cup (1 stick) unsalted butter

2 tablespoons chopped pistachios

1 tablespoon finely chopped fresh tarragon

Kosher or sea salt and freshly ground black pepper to taste

2 pounds large sea scallops

METHOD

1. Prepare a hot fire in a grill. Oil 2 cast-iron skillets or a cast-iron grill griddle and preheat on the grill.

2. To make the brown butter, melt the butter in a saucepan over medium-high heat. Keep cooking until the butter starts to bubble and turn a medium brown and has a nutty aroma, 3 to 5 minutes. (Do not let the butter get too dark.) Remove from the heat and stir in the pistachios and tarragon. Season to taste with salt and pepper. Pour 1 to 2 tablespoons of the melted pistachio butter into a ramekin to use on the raw scallops while grilling. Reserve the rest of the butter mixture as a serving sauce; keep warm.

3. Brush the sea scallops with the melted butter mixture from the ramekin and place on the prepared grill rack or griddle. Grill for about 3 minutes before turning. If the scallops stick, cook them a little longer, until they turn easily. After turning, grill long enough to heat through, 1 to 2 more minutes.

4. Drizzle the seared scallops with the reserved warm pistachio-tarragon brown butter and serve.

CHAR-GRILLED SQUID IN SHERRY MARINADE

SERVES 4

Cut into rings and tentacles and deep fried, squid have claimed a top spot on restaurant appetizer menus as calamari. But why go out for calamari when you can grill them at home? Whole, marinated squid, done to a turn on your grill, can transform your backyard into a tapas bar. Just stir up a pitcher of sangria or chill a bottle of fino sherry, and you're good to go.

The technique you use for grilling squid is the same as for whole baby octopus or cut-up octopus tentacles. You want to marinate them first to imbue them with flavor. Squid and octopus are not as delicate as fish, so you can marinate them longer—ideally, for 3 to 4 hours. Then, grill them quickly on an oiled, perforated grill rack (so they don't fall through the grill grates) over a hot fire; that way, they crisp up without getting rubbery.

INGREDIENTS

SHERRY MARINADE

¼ cup olive oil

¼ cup dry sherry

6 cloves garlic, minced

1 tablespoon dried oregano

1 teaspoon red pepper flakes

1 teaspoon paprika

½ teaspoon salt

1½ to 2 pounds squid (or baby octopus), cleaned, long tentacles trimmed if desired

Extra-virgin olive oil

Chopped fresh flat-leaf parsley for garnish

METHOD

1. To make the marinade, whisk all the ingredients together in a large bowl. Add the squid, cover, and let marinate in the refrigerator for 3 to 4 hours.

2. Prepare a hot fire in a grill. Oil a perforated grill rack or a cast-iron grill griddle and preheat on the grill.

3. Remove the squid from the marinade. Place the squid on the prepared grill rack and grill for 4 minutes, turning once, or until the squid are almost opaque all the way through and have crisped around the ends and tentacles. Do not overcook or they will become rubbery.

4. To serve, arrange on a platter, drizzle with olive oil, and scatter with parsley.

AUSSIE-GRILLED PRAWNS ON THE BARBIE

SERVES 4

Prawns can be a type of shellfish, like the Italian *scampi* or the French *langoustine* or the Florida lobsterette. "Prawn" can also refer to just a large shrimp. Confused yet? No matter. For this recipe, just look for the largest shrimp or prawns you can find, such as the Alaska spot prawn, known as "the lobster of Alaska." They're usually sold fresh in the seafood case, not frozen. Large prawns can range from 10 to a pound to about 1 pound each. If they have their heads on, leave them on, as this contributes to the flavor. You can always remove the heads after grilling if you or your dinner guests are squeamish.

Grill the prawns quickly on an oiled, perforated grill rack (so they don't fall through the grill grates) over a hot fire, basting as you go with an Aussie-inspired basting sauce that blends Asian flavors of soy and ginger with white wine. You can't help but have a "g'day, mate" when you sit down to this dish.

INGREDIENTS

AUSSIE BASTING SAUCE

1½ cups dry white wine, such as Australian Chardonnay

2 tablespoons rice wine vinegar

2 tablespoons grated fresh ginger

2 large shallots, minced

1 cup (2 sticks) unsalted butter, chilled and cut into cubes

1 tablespoon soy sauce

½ teaspoon toasted sesame oil

12 prawns, 2 to 3 ounces each or larger, peeled and deveined

4 heads baby bok choy, ends trimmed and sliced in half lengthwise

Kosher or sea salt and freshly ground black pepper to taste

METHOD

1. Prepare a hot fire in your grill.

2. To make the sauce, bring the wine, rice wine vinegar, ginger, and shallots to a boil in a saucepan over high heat and reduce until only 2 tablespoons of liquid remain, 7 to 10 minutes. Remove from the heat and whisk in the butter, a cube at a time, until the sauce has emulsified. (If it starts to separate, whisk in an ice cube and keep whisking until the sauce comes back together.) Whisk in the soy sauce and sesame oil. Transfer ¼ cup of the basting sauce to a ramekin to use for basting. Reserve the rest for serving; keep warm.

3. Brush the prawns and baby bok choy with the basting sauce from the ramekin and season with salt and pepper. Place the prawns on the grill grate and grill for about 3 minutes before turning. If the prawns stick, cook them a little longer, until they turn easily. After turning, grill long enough to heat through, about 2 minutes. Grill the baby bok choy on the cut side for 1 to 2 minutes, or until the exterior has grill marks and the interior is still crisp.

4. Arrange 2 bok choy halves on each of 4 plates, then arrange 3 prawns on each plate. Spoon the reserved sauce over all and serve.

DOUBLE-SKEWERED SHRIMP AND SCALLOPS

SERVES 4

This is a perfect tidbit with cocktails, with one shrimp and one scallop threaded at the end of a double skewer for easy-eating finger food. The skewered shrimp curl around each scallop, making this dish exceptionally good-looking, too.

Double skewering is a technique using two parallel skewers to hold small items of food in place that might normally twirl around on a single skewer. This works well with chunks of vegetables or meat as well as seafood. The least expensive option is to use wooden skewers soaked in water for at least 30 minutes. Lay the skewers side by side and thread the shrimp and scallops on both skewers at the same time. Don't overload the skewers or push the food too close together; a little spacing allows for more even cooking. Double metal skewers are another choice. Or you could cheat a little and buy flat metal skewers. If using flat skewers, you usually do not need to double them, as the flat spear keeps food from twirling.

INGREDIENTS

Grated zest and juice of 2 lemons

Juice of ½ orange

¼ cup orange-flavored liqueur, such as Grand Marnier

8 giant sea scallops (about 1 pound)

8 jumbo shrimp (about 1 pound), peeled and deveined

16 wooden skewers, soaked in water for at least 30 minutes

1 cucumber, thinly sliced, for garnish

2 oranges, thinly sliced, for garnish

METHOD

1. Combine the lemon juice and zest, orange juice, and liqueur in a large bowl. Add the scallops and shrimp. Cover and marinate for 1 to 2 hours in the refrigerator.

2. Prepare a hot fire in your grill.

3. Drain the marinade into a small saucepan and boil for 5 minutes to reuse for basting.

4. Thread the scallops and shrimp alternately onto 8 double skewers so that each shrimp curls around a scallop. Keep the shellfish toward the end of the skewers.

5. Place the skewered shellfish directly over the fire. Grill for 6 to 8 minutes, turning 3 or 4 times during grilling so that you can baste both sides a couple of times with the reserved boiled marinade.

6. Overlap the cucumber and orange slices on a platter. Place the grilled shrimp and scallop skewers on top, and serve.

STIR-GRILLED SHRIMP AND RED CABBAGE PO' BOYS

SERVES 4

This is a spicy grilled version of the traditionally fried New Orleans–style sandwich. Medium to large shrimp, peeled and deveined, work best in this stir-grilled recipe. Extra-large shrimp can be used, but you'll need to cut them to fit into the sandwich bun for easier eating.

Once the shrimp is almost done, we throw the cabbage into the grill wok to give it a little bit of heat. Yes, grilled cabbage is wonderful. We even grill wedges of cabbage and then chop them up for some good charry flavor in coleslaw!

A store-bought spicy Creole-style rub can also be sprinkled on the shrimp before they are tossed in the grill basket or wok. These spicy shrimp on their own would be a great addition to a cobb or niçoise salad.

INGREDIENTS

1 pound medium to large shrimp, peeled and deveined

2 teaspoons olive oil

1 teaspoon ground ancho chile powder

½ teaspoon smoked paprika

½ teaspoon freshly ground black pepper

¼ teaspoon kosher salt

2 cups finely shredded red cabbage

½ cup Homemade Tartar Sauce (page 22)

4 hoagie buns, split and brushed with olive oil

4 tomato slices, halved crosswise

4 thin red onion slices, halved crosswise

METHOD

1. Prepare a hot fire in your grill. Oil both sides of a perforated grill basket or wok.

2. Combine the shrimp, oil, ground chile, smoked paprika, black pepper, and salt in a large bowl. Toss to coat.

3. Pour the seasoned shrimp into the grill basket or wok and set directly over the hot fire. Toss with long-handled tongs or wooden spoons until shrimp are almost done, about 3 minutes. Then pour the cabbage into the wok and stir-grill the cabbage and the shrimp for 1 to 2 minutes. Pour all into a large bowl and dress with the tartar sauce, tossing to blend. Set aside.

4. Grill the buns on both sides until crisp, about 30 seconds per side.

5. For each po' boy, place 2 pieces of tomato on one side of the grilled bun. Place 2 pieces of red onion on the other side. Spoon the dressed shrimp and cabbage down the middle of each sandwich. Serve immediately.

PLANKED SCALLOPS WITH BÉARNAISE BUTTER

SERVES 4

Baking (or roasting) planks are thicker than grilling planks and have a hollowed-out center that is great for holding sauces or butters that would run off a flat grilling plank. They are available at kitchen shops, barbecue stores, and online. Remember to soak them in water for at least 1 hour before planking.

Here scallops (or you could use shrimp) are arranged in a single layer on the plank to expose the most food surface to the wood. This lends the maximum wood flavor to the scallops. Instead of the béarnaise butter, try your hand at making your own compound butter by adding a combination of one or more flavors to melted butter, like garlic, hot sauce, citrus juice, chopped fresh ginger, or chopped fresh herbs.

INGREDIENTS

BÉARNAISE BUTTER

2 tablespoons chopped fresh shallot

1 tablespoon white wine vinegar

2 tablespoons chopped fresh tarragon

¼ teaspoon kosher or sea salt

½ teaspoon hot pepper sauce, or to taste

½ cup (1 stick) unsalted butter, softened

16 large sea scallops, ¾ to 1 pound

1 cedar or alder baking plank, soaked in water for at least 1 hour

1 baguette, sliced

METHOD

1. Prepare an indirect fire in your grill, with a hot fire on one side and no fire on the other.

2. To make the butter, combine the shallot and vinegar in a small saucepan. Bring to a boil, and then remove from the heat. Add the tarragon, salt, hot pepper sauce, and butter. Stir to blend and melt the butter.

3. Place the scallops in the hollow groove of the baking plank. Drizzle half the butter over the scallops. Place the plank on the no-fire side of the grill and close the lid. Cook for about 20 minutes, or until the scallops are beginning to turn opaque. Open the lid and cook for another 2 or 3 minutes, to the desired doneness. Then remove the plank from the grill.

4. Serve the scallops from the plank with the remaining butter on the side for dipping and the baguette for soaking up the additional sauce.

BASIL-PROSCIUTTO AND SPINACH-BRIE GRILLED SHRIMP

SERVES 6

Why wrap? Because our technique is easy, and the wrapping is not only delicious but also keeps the shellfish fragrant and moist. The wrapping does not stay perfectly in place during cooking, so there's no point in painstakingly trying to make each wrapped shrimp look like you went to French culinary camp. This is grilling, and it is supposed to be easy and fun. But, if you are really a neatnik, you can thread the wrapped shrimp onto a skewer to keep the wrappings in place.

The prosciutto and basil–wrapped shrimp take on a little bit of char, while the Brie and spinach–wrapped shrimp get deliciously oozy. The naked shrimp add their beautiful pink color to the serving platter (and it is less work to leave a few of the shrimp unadorned). Other wrappings you could try include thin slices of bacon or large leaves of arugula; you could substitute lemon balm, a tender mint leaf, or a few oregano leaves for the basil. You could even stuff the shrimp with a bit of Boursin before you wrap them.

INGREDIENTS

18 jumbo shrimp, about 1 pound, peeled and deveined

3 thin slices prosciutto, cut in half lengthwise

6 fresh basil leaves

6 to 12 large spinach leaves

6 small slices Brie (about 1 x 1½ x ⅛ inches each)

Olive oil for drizzling

METHOD

1. Prepare a medium-hot fire in your grill. Oil both sides of a perforated grill rack and set atop a baking sheet.

2. Set 6 of the shrimp on the oiled grill rack, leaving them plain. For the next 6 shrimp, spread out 1 slice of prosciutto and place 1 basil leaf at the end of the slice; place 1 shrimp on top of the basil. Roll the shrimp in the prosciutto and set them on the grill rack. For the remaining 6 shrimp, spread out 1 or 2 spinach leaves and place 1 slice of cheese on top of the spinach (spinach leaves vary so much in size that you may need to use 2 to cover the shrimp); place 1 shrimp on top of the cheese. Fold the spinach leaf over the shrimp, turn the shrimp over, and set them on the grill rack. Then lightly drizzle all with olive oil.

3. Set the grill rack of shrimp directly over the fire and close the lid. Grill for about 3 minutes, then open the lid and turn the shrimp once; continue to grill. When the naked shrimp are opaque (after about 3 more minutes), take them off the grill. Grill the wrapped shrimp for another 1 to 2 minutes and arrange all on a platter. Serve warm.

MEASUREMENT EQUIVALENTS

LIQUID CONVERSIONS

U.S.	Metric
1 tsp	5 ml
1 tbs	15 ml
2 tbs	30 ml
3 tbs	45 ml
1/4 cup	60 ml
1/3 cup	75 ml
1/3 cup + 1 tbs	90 ml
1/3 cup + 2 tbs	100 ml
1/2 cup	120 ml
2/3 cup	150 ml
3/4 cup	180 ml
3/4 cup + 2 tbs	200 ml
1 cup	240 ml
1 cup + 2 tbs	275 ml
1 1/4 cups	300 ml
1 1/3 cups	325 ml
1 1/2 cups	350 ml
1 2/3 cups	375 ml
1 3/4 cups	400 ml
1 3/4 cups + 2 tbs	450 ml
2 cups (1 pint)	475 ml
2 1/2 cups	600 ml
3 cups	720 ml
4 cups (1 quart)	945 ml

(1,000 ml is 1 liter)

WEIGHT CONVERSIONS

U.S./U.K.	Metric
1/2 oz	14 g
1 oz	28 g
1 1/2 oz	43 g
2 oz	57 g
2 1/2 oz	71 g
3 oz	85 g
3 1/2 oz	100 g
4 oz	113 g
5 oz	142 g
6 oz	170 g
7 oz	200 g
8 oz	227 g
9 oz	255 g
10 oz	284 g
11 oz	312 g
12 oz	340 g
13 oz	368 g
14 oz	400 g
15 oz	425 g
1 lb	454 g

OVEN TEMPERATURE CONVERSIONS

°F	Gas Mark	°C
250	½	120
275	1	140
300	2	150
325	3	165
350	4	180
375	5	190
400	6	200
425	7	220
450	8	230
475	9	240
500	10	260
550	Broil	290

NOTE: All conversions are approximate

RESOURCES

BARBECUE AND GRILL MANUFACTURERS

BIG GREEN EGG
3417 Lawrenceville Highway
Tucker, GA 30084-5802
(770) 934-5300
www.biggreenegg.com
Large producer of an egg-shaped, ceramic kamado combination smoker/grill that cooks at a higher temperature than traditional cookers.

CHAR-BROIL/W.C. BRADLEY
P.O. Box 1240
Columbus, GA 31902
(866) 239-6777
www.charbroil.com
Manufacturer of gas and electric grills and barbecue accessories. Also the maker of the New Braunfels heavy-gauge steel smokers and grills.

HASTY-BAKE
1313 S. Lewis Avenue
Tulsa, OK 74104
(800) 426-6836
www.hastybake.com
Manufacturer of the Hasty-Bake oven, a charcoal grill/smoker that has a crank system to raise and lower the grill grates over the fire. Side door for refueling is nifty, too.

KITCHENAID
P.O. Box 218
St. Joseph, MI 49085
(800) 422-1230
www.kitchenaid.com
Major appliance manufacturer of, among other products, outdoor cooking systems, refrigeration products, and refreshment systems.

VIKING RANGE CORPORATION
111 Front Street
Greenwood, MS 38930
(888) 845-4641
www.vikingrange.com
Manufacturer of stainless-steel gas grill outdoor kitchens and professional-quality appliances for the home.

WEBER-STEPHEN PRODUCTS COMPANY

200 East Daniels Road
Palatine, IL 60067-6266
(800) 446-1071
www.weber.com
Manufacturer of the original Weber grill since 1952. Grills, smokers, and all their accessories, as well as the Weber Smokey Mountain Cooker, a charcoal chimney starter, and more.

WOOD PRODUCTS AND PLANKS

BARBECUEWOOD.COM

P.O. Box 8163
Yakima, WA 98908
(800) 379-9663
www.barbecuewood.com
A variety of wood grilling and baking planks in alder, cherry, cedar, maple, white oak, and hickory. Also wood chunks and chips in hard-to-find varieties such as apricot, as well as all the usual woods used for smoking.

BBQR'S DELIGHT

P.O. Box 8727
1609 Celia Road
Pine Bluff, AR 71601
(877) 275-9591
www.bbqrsdelight.com
Compressed wood pellets for fuel and smoke in hickory, mesquite, pecan, apple, cherry, oak, black walnut, mulberry, orange, Jack Daniel's, sugar maple, and more.

CHIGGER CREEK PRODUCTS

4200 Highway D
Syracuse, MO 65354
(660) 298-3188
www.chiggercreekproducts.net
Hardwood lump charcoal, as well as a variety of woods: hickory, apple, cherry, pecan, grape, sugar maple, alder, oak, mesquite, peach, sassafras, persimmon, pear, apple-hickory and cherry-oak blends, in chips, chunks, and logs.

FIRE & FLAVOR

375 #B Commerce Boulevard
Bogart, GA 30622
(866) 728-8332
www.fireandflavor.com
Aromatic western red cedar grilling planks. Custom packing available.

NATURE'S CUISINE

#6 - 8444 Aitken Road
Chilliwack, BC
Canada V2R 3W8
(866) 977-5265
www.natures-cuisine.com
Cedar, alder, and maple oven-roasting planks. Wide variety of grill planks, too.

WW WOOD

1799 Corgey Road
P.O. Box 398
Pleasanton, TX 78064
(830) 569-2501
www.woodinc.com
Smoking and grilling woods.

BARBECUE BOOKS, NEWSLETTERS, AND CLASSES

BBQ QUEENS

www.bbqqueens.com
Official online site of the BBQ Queens, Karen Adler and Judith Fertig. Features tips and recipes for outdoor cooking, culinary classes taught by the BBQ Queens, and information about their books.

KANSAS CITY BULLSHEET

Kansas City Barbeque Society
11514 Hickman Mills Drive
Kansas City, MO 64134
(800) 963-5227
www.kcbs.us
Monthly newspaper published by the Kansas City Barbeque Society, featuring everything barbecue.

NATIONAL BARBECUE NEWS

P.O. Box 981
Douglas, GA 31534-0981
(800) 385-0002
www.barbecuenews.com
Monthly newspaper featuring barbecue events and columns. Also the official newspaper of the National Barbecue Association.

PIG OUT PUBLICATIONS, INC.

6005 Martway, Suite 107
Mission, KS 66202
(800) 877-3119
www.pigoutpublications.com
BBQ Queen Karen Adler owns this company, which offers more than 200 barbecue cookbooks.

INDEX

ABOUT THE AUTHORS

KAREN ADLER and JUDITH FERTIG are the BBQ Queens and have been spreading the word on slow-smoked barbecue and hot-and-fast grilling throughout the country in magazine and newspaper articles, cooking classes, and television and radio guest appearances, and at special events. Karen has her M.B. (master of barbecue philosophy), Judith holds membership in the Order of the Magic Mop, and both have their Ph.B. (doctor of barbecue philosophy) degrees, all awarded by the Kansas City Barbeque Society's prestigious Greasehouse University, founded by Ardie A. Davis.

As cookbook authors, they've cumulatively written more than 20 cookbooks, including *Fish & Shellfish, Grilled & Smoked*; *Weeknight Grilling with the BBQ Queens*; and *BBQ Bash*. They have appeared on the Food Network's *Grill Gals* special and on PBS. They have been featured in *Food & Wine, Bon Appétit, Southern Living*, and many other publications. Both Queens are culinary instructors and have taught thousands of students the secrets of grilling, smoking, planking, and cooking fish and shellfish. Visit their website at www.bbqqueens.com.